50th Annual Meeting of the Association for Computational Linguistics 2012 (ACL 2012)

Tutorial Abstracts

Jeju Island, Korea
8-14 July 2012

ISBN: 978-1-62276-276-7

Printed from e-media with permission by:

Curran Associates, Inc.
57 Morehouse Lane
Red Hook, NY 12571

Some format issues inherent in the e-media version may also appear in this print version.

Printed by Curran Associates, Inc. (2012)

For permission requests, please contact the Association for Computational Linguistics
at the address below.

Association for Computational Linguistics
209 N. Eighth Street
Stroudsburg, Pennsylvania 18360

Phone: 1-570-476-8006
Fax: 1-570-476-0860

acl@aclweb.org

Additional copies of this publication are available from:

Curran Associates, Inc.
57 Morehouse Lane
Red Hook, NY 12571 USA
Phone: 845-758-0400
Fax: 845-758-2634
Email: curran@proceedings.com
Web: www.proceedings.com

Introduction

A total of 17 tutorial proposals were submitted to the ACL 2012 Tutorials track from which six were finally accepted. I am grateful to the ACL community for the diverse, and high-quality proposals I received. This guarantees a strong tutorials track at ACL 2012, but at the same time made the selection process very difficult. All 17 proposals were reviewed by the chair with assistance by colleagues and experts from the NLP community where necessary. The final selection was approved by the ACL 2012 General Chair.

The following criteria guided the selection: (1) Quality: content, scope and organization of the proposal, competence and experience of the presenters. (2) Diversity: I tried to include diverse topics ranging from linguistically motivated approaches to current developments in machine learning. (3) Novelty: Tutorials recently held at ACL events were not selected.

One of my aims was to convince the presenters that they make their tutorials accessible to the novice in the respective areas. In my acceptance email I told them: "When preparing for the tutorial, please keep in mind that the target audience is not your buddies whom you may want to impress, but researchers and graduate students who are not familiar with your topic."

I would like to thank all the presenters for putting a lot of effort in the tutorials. I am indebted to the Local Chairs, the Publication Chairs and the ACL 2012 General Chair for making it happen.

Enjoy,

Michael Strube, HITS gGmbH
ACL 2012 Tutorial Chair

Tutorial Chair:

Michael Strube
Heidelberg Institute for Theoretical Studies, gGmbH
Heidelberg, Germany

Table of Contents

Tutorial Program

Sunday July 8, 2012

Morning

9:00-12:30	*Qualitative Modeling of Spatial Prepositions and Motion Expressions* Inderjeet Mani and James Pustejovsky
	State-of-the-Art Kernels for Natural Language Processing Alessandro Moschitti
	Topic Models, Latent Space Models, Sparse Coding, and All That: A Systematic Understanding of Probabilistic Semantic Extraction in Large Corpus Eric Xing
12:30-2:00	Lunch Break

Afternoon

2:00-5:30	*Multilingual Subjectivity and Sentiment Analysis* Rada Mihalcea, Carmen Banea and Janyce Wiebe
	Deep Learning for NLP (without Magic) Richard Socher, Yoshua Bengio and Christopher D. Manning
	Graph-based Semi-Supervised Learning Algorithms for NLP Amar Subramanya and Partha Pratim Talukdar

Qualitative Modeling of Spatial Prepositions and Motion Expressions

Inderjeet Mani
Children's Organization of
Southeast Asia
Thailand
inderjeet.mani@gmail.com

James Pustejovsky
Computer Science Department
Brandeis University
Waltham, MA USA
jamesp@cs.brandeis.edu

The ability to understand spatial prepositions and motion in natural language will enable a variety of new applications involving systems that can respond to verbal directions, map travel guides, display incident reports, etc., providing for enhanced information extraction, question-answering, information retrieval, and more principled text to scene rendering. Until now, however, the semantics of spatial relations and motion verbs has been highly problematic. This tutorial presents a new approach to the semantics of spatial descriptions and motion expressions based on linguistically interpreted qualitative reasoning. Our approach allows for formal inference from spatial descriptions in natural language, while leveraging annotation schemes for time, space, and motion, along with machine learning from annotated corpora. We introduce a compositional semantics for motion expressions that integrates spatial primitives drawn from qualitative calculi.

No previous exposure to the semantics of spatial prepositions or motion verbs is assumed. The tutorial will sharpen cross-linguistic intuitions about the interpretation of spatial prepositions and motion constructions. The attendees will also learn about qualitative reasoning schemes for static and dynamic spatial information, as well as three annotation schemes: TimeML, SpatialML, and ISO-Space, for time, space, and motion, respectively.

While both cognitive and formal linguistics have examined the meaning of motion verbs and spatial prepositions, these earlier approaches do not yield precise computable representations that are expressive enough for natural languages. However, the previous literature makes it clear that communication of motion relies on imprecise and highly abstract geometric descriptions, rather than Euclidean ones that specify the coordinates and shapes of every object. This property makes these expressions a fit target for the field of qualitative spatial reasoning in AI, which has developed a rich set of geometric primitives for representing time, space (including distance, orientation, and topological relations), and motion. The results of such research have yielded a wide variety of spatial and temporal reasoning logics and tools. By reviewing these calculi and resources, this tutorial aims to systematically connect qualitative reasoning to natural language.

Tutorial Schedule:

I. Introduction. i. Overview of geometric idealizations underlying spatial PPs; ii. Linguistic patterns of motion verbs across languages; iii. A qualitative model for static spatial descriptions and for path verbs; iv. Overview of relevant annotation schemes.

II. Calculi for Qualitative Spatial Reasoning. i. Semantics of spatial PPs mapped to qualitative spatial reasoning; ii. Qualitative calculi for representing topological and orientation relations; iii. Qualitative calculi to represent motion.

III. Semantics of Motion Expressions. i. Introduction to Dynamic Interval Temporal Logic (DITL); ii. DITL representations for manner-of-motion verbs and path verbs; iii. Compositional semantics for motion expressions in DITL, with the spatial primitives drawn from qualitative calculi.

IV. Applications and Research Topics. i. Route navigation, mapping travel narratives, QA, scene rendering from text, and generating event descriptions; ii. Open issues and further research topics.

Tutorial Abstracts of ACL 2012, page 1,
Jeju, Republic of Korea, 8 July 2012. ©2012 Association for Computational Linguistics

State-of-the-Art Kernels for Natural Language Processing

Alessandro Moschitti
Department of Computer Science and Information Engineering
University of Trento
Via Sommarive 5, 38123 Povo (TN), Italy
moschitti@disi.unitn.it

Introduction

In recent years, machine learning (ML) has been used more and more to solve complex tasks in different disciplines, ranging from Data Mining to Information Retrieval or Natural Language Processing (NLP). These tasks often require the processing of structured input, e.g., the ability to extract salient features from syntactic/semantic structures is critical to many NLP systems. Mapping such structured data into explicit feature vectors for ML algorithms requires large expertise, intuition and deep knowledge about the target linguistic phenomena. Kernel Methods (KM) are powerful ML tools (see e.g., (Shawe-Taylor and Cristianini, 2004)), which can alleviate the data representation problem. They substitute feature-based similarities with similarity functions, i.e., kernels, directly defined between training/test instances, e.g., syntactic trees. Hence feature vectors are not needed any longer. Additionally, kernel engineering, i.e., the composition or adaptation of several prototype kernels, facilitates the design of effective similarities required for new tasks, e.g., (Moschitti, 2004; Moschitti, 2008).

Tutorial Content

The tutorial aims at addressing the problems above: firstly, it will introduce essential and simplified theory of Support Vector Machines and KM with the only aim of motivating practical procedures and interpreting the results. Secondly, it will simply describe the current best practices for designing applications based on effective kernels. For this purpose, it will survey state-of-the-art kernels for diverse NLP applications, reconciling the different approaches with a uniform and global notation/theory. Such survey will benefit from practical expertise acquired from directly working on many natural language applications, ranging from Text Categorization to Syntactic/Semantic Parsing. Moreover, practical demonstrations using SVM-Light-TK toolkit will nicely support the application-oriented perspective of the tutorial. The latter will lead NLP researchers with heterogeneous background to the acquisition of the KM know-how, which can be used to design any target NLP application.

Finally, the tutorial will propose interesting new best practices, e.g., some recent methods for large-scale learning with structural kernels (Severyn and Moschitti, 2011), structural lexical similarities (Croce et al., 2011) and reverse kernel engineering (Pighin and Moschitti, 2009).

References

Danilo Croce, Alessandro Moschitti, and Roberto Basili. 2011. Structured Lexical Similarity via Convolution Kernels on Dependency Trees. In *Proc. of EMNLP*.

Alessandro Moschitti. 2004. A Study on Convolution Kernels for Shallow Semantic Parsing. In *Proceedings of ACL*.

Alessandro Moschitti. 2008. Kernel Methods, Syntax and Semantics for Relational Text Categorization. In *Proceedings of CIKM*.

Daniele Pighin and Alessandro Moschitti. 2009. Efficient Linearization of Tree Kernel Functions. In *Proceedings of CoNLL*.

Aliaksei Severyn and Alessandro Moschitti. 2011. Fast Support Vector Machines for Structural Kernels. In *ECML*.

John Shawe-Taylor and Nello Cristianini. 2004. *Kernel Methods for Pattern Analysis*. Cambridge Univ. Press.

Tutorial Abstracts of ACL 2012, page 2,
Jeju, Republic of Korea, 8 July 2012. ©2012 Association for Computational Linguistics

Topic Models, Latent Space Models, Sparse Coding, and All That: A systematic understanding of probabilistic semantic extraction in large corpus

Eric Xing
School of Computer Science
Carnegie Mellon University

Abstract

Probabilistic topic models have recently gained much popularity in informational retrieval and related areas. Via such models, one can project high-dimensional objects such as text documents into a low dimensional space where their latent semantics are captured and modeled; can integrate multiple sources of information—to "share statistical strength" among components of a hierarchical probabilistic model; and can structurally display and classify the otherwise unstructured object collections. However, to many practitioners, how topic models work, what to and not to expect from a topic model, how is it different from and related to classical matrix algebraic techniques such as LSI, NMF in NLP, how to empower topic models to deal with complex scenarios such as multimodal data, contractual text in social media, evolving corpus, or presence of supervision such as labeling and rating, how to make topic modeling computationally tractable even on web-scale data, etc., in a principled way, remain unclear. In this tutorial, I will demystify the conceptual, mathematical, and computational issues behind all such problems surrounding the topic models and their applications by presenting a systematic overview of the mathematical foundation of topic modeling, and its connections to a number of related methods popular in other fields such as the LDA, admixture model, mixed membership model, latent space models, and sparse coding. I will offer a simple and unifying view of all these techniques under the framework multi-view latent space embedding, and online the roadmap of model extension and algorithmic design toward different applications in IR and NLP. A main theme of this tutorial that tie together a wide range of issues and problems will build on the "probabilistic graphical model" formalism, a formalism that exploits the conjoined talents of graph theory and probability theory to build complex models out of simpler pieces. I will use this formalism as a main aid to discuss both the mathematical underpinnings for the models and the related computational issues in a unified, simplistic, transparent, and actionable fashion.

Tutorial Abstracts of ACL 2012, page 3,
Jeju, Republic of Korea, 8 July 2012.

Multilingual Subjectivity and Sentiment Analysis

Rada Mihalcea
University of North Texas
Denton, Tx
rada@cs.unt.edu

Carmen Banea
University of North Texas
Denton, Tx
carmenbanea@my.unt.edu

Janyce Wiebe
University of Pittsburgh
Pittsburgh, Pa
wiebe@cs.pitt.edu

Abstract

Subjectivity and sentiment analysis focuses on the automatic identification of private states, such as opinions, emotions, sentiments, evaluations, beliefs, and speculations in natural language. While subjectivity classification labels text as either subjective or objective, sentiment classification adds an additional level of granularity, by further classifying subjective text as either positive, negative or neutral.

While much of the research work in this area has been applied to English, research on other languages is growing, including Japanese, Chinese, German, Spanish, Romanian. While most of the researchers in the field are familiar with the methods applied on English, few of them have closely looked at the original research carried out in other languages. For example, in languages such as Chinese, researchers have been looking at the ability of characters to carry sentiment information (Ku et al., 2005; Xiang, 2011). In Romanian, due to markers of politeness and additional verbal modes embedded in the language, experiments have hinted that subjectivity detection may be easier to achieve (Banea et al., 2008). These additional sources of information may not be available across all languages, yet, various articles have pointed out that by investigating a synergistic approach for detecting subjectivity and sentiment in multiple languages at the same time, improvements can be achieved not only in other languages, but in English as well. The development and interest in these methods is also highly motivated by the fact that only 27% of Internet users speak English (www.internetworldstats.com/stats.htm, Oct 11, 2011), and that number diminishes further every year, as more people across the globe gain Internet access.

The aim of this tutorial is to familiarize the attendees with the subjectivity and sentiment research carried out on languages other than English in order to enable and promote cross-fertilization. Specifically, we will review work along three main directions. First, we will present methods where the resources and tools have been specifically developed for a given target language. In this category, we will also briefly overview the main methods that have been proposed for English, but which can be easily ported to other languages. Second, we will describe cross-lingual approaches, including several methods that have been proposed to leverage on the resources and tools available in English by using cross-lingual projections. Finally, third, we will show how the expression of opinions and polarity pervades language boundaries, and thus methods that holistically explore multiple languages at the same time can be effectively considered.

References

C. Banea, R. Mihalcea, and J. Wiebe. 2008. A Bootstrapping method for building subjectivity lexicons for languages with scarce resources. In *Proceedings of LREC 2008*, Marrakech, Morocco.

L. W. Ku, T. H. Wu, L. Y. Lee, and H. H. Chen. 2005. Construction of an Evaluation Corpus for Opinion Extraction. In *Proceedings of NTCIR-5*, Tokyo, Japan.

L. Xiang. 2011. Ideogram Based Chinese Sentiment Word Orientation Computation. *Computing Research Repository*, page 4, October.

Tutorial Abstracts of ACL 2012, page 4,
Jeju, Republic of Korea, 8 July 2012.

Deep Learning for NLP (without Magic)

Richard Socher   Yoshua Bengio[*]   Christopher D. Manning
richard@socher.org   bengioy@iro.umontreal.ca, manning@stanford.edu
Computer Science Department, Stanford University
[*] DIRO, Université de Montréal, Montréal, QC, Canada

1 Abtract

Machine learning is everywhere in today's NLP, but by and large machine learning amounts to numerical optimization of weights for human designed representations and features. The goal of deep learning is to explore how computers can take advantage of data to develop features and representations appropriate for complex interpretation tasks. This tutorial aims to cover the basic motivation, ideas, models and learning algorithms in deep learning for natural language processing. Recently, these methods have been shown to perform very well on various NLP tasks such as language modeling, POS tagging, named entity recognition, sentiment analysis and paraphrase detection, among others. The most attractive quality of these techniques is that they can perform well without any external hand-designed resources or time-intensive feature engineering. Despite these advantages, many researchers in NLP are not familiar with these methods. Our focus is on insight and understanding, using graphical illustrations and simple, intuitive derivations. The goal of the tutorial is to make the inner workings of these techniques transparent, intuitive and their results interpretable, rather than black boxes labeled "magic here".

The first part of the tutorial presents the basics of neural networks, neural word vectors, several simple models based on local windows and the math and algorithms of training via backpropagation. In this section applications include language modeling and POS tagging.

In the second section we present recursive neural networks which can learn structured tree outputs as well as vector representations for phrases and sentences. We cover both equations as well as applications. We show how training can be achieved by a modified version of the backpropagation algorithm introduced before. These modifications allow the algorithm to work on tree structures. Applications include sentiment analysis and paraphrase detection. We also draw connections to recent work in semantic compositionality in vector spaces. The principle goal, again, is to make these methods appear intuitive and interpretable rather than mathematically confusing. By this point in the tutorial, the audience members should have a clear understanding of how to build a deep learning system for word-, sentence- and document-level tasks.

The last part of the tutorial gives a general overview of the different applications of deep learning in NLP, including bag of words models. We will provide a discussion of NLP-oriented issues in modeling, interpretation, representational power, and optimization.

Tutorial Abstracts of ACL 2012, page 5,
Jeju, Republic of Korea, 8 July 2012.

Graph-based Semi-Supervised Learning Algorithms for NLP

Amar Subramanya
Google Research
asubram@google.com

Partha Pratim Talukdar
Carnegie Mellon University
ppt@cs.cmu.edu

Abstract

While labeled data is expensive to prepare, ever increasing amounts of unlabeled linguistic data are becoming widely available. In order to adapt to this phenomenon, several semi-supervised learning (SSL) algorithms, which learn from labeled as well as unlabeled data, have been developed. In a separate line of work, researchers have started to realize that graphs provide a natural way to represent data in a variety of domains. Graph-based SSL algorithms, which bring together these two lines of work, have been shown to outperform the state-of-the-art in many applications in speech processing, computer vision and NLP. In particular, recent NLP research has successfully used graph-based SSL algorithms for PoS tagging (Subramanya et al., 2010), semantic parsing (Das and Smith, 2011), knowledge acquisition (Talukdar et al., 2008), sentiment analysis (Goldberg and Zhu, 2006) and text categorization (Subramanya and Bilmes, 2008).

Recognizing this promising and emerging area of research, this tutorial focuses on graph-based SSL algorithms (e.g., label propagation methods). The tutorial is intended to be a sequel to the ACL 2008 SSL tutorial, focusing exclusively on graph-based SSL methods and recent advances in this area, which were beyond the scope of the previous tutorial.

The tutorial is divided in two parts. In the first part, we will motivate the need for graph-based SSL methods, introduce some standard graph-based SSL algorithms, and discuss connections between these approaches. We will also discuss how linguistic data can be encoded as graphs and show how graph-based algorithms can be scaled to large amounts of data (e.g., web-scale data).

Part 2 of the tutorial will focus on how graph-based methods can be used to solve several critical NLP tasks, including basic problems such as PoS tagging, semantic parsing, and more downstream tasks such as text categorization, information acquisition, and sentiment analysis. We will conclude the tutorial with some exciting avenues for future work.

Familiarity with semi-supervised learning and graph-based methods will not be assumed, and the necessary background will be provided. Examples from NLP tasks will be used throughout the tutorial to convey the necessary concepts. At the end of this tutorial, the attendee will walk away with the following:

- An in-depth knowledge of the current state-of-the-art in graph-based SSL algorithms, and the ability to implement them.
- The ability to decide on the suitability of graph-based SSL methods for a problem.
- Familiarity with different NLP tasks where graph-based SSL methods have been successfully applied.

In addition to the above goals, we hope that this tutorial will better prepare the attendee to conduct exciting research at the intersection of NLP and other emerging areas with natural graph-structured data (e.g., Computation Social Science).

Please visit http://graph-ssl.wikidot.com/ for details.

References

Dipanjan Das and Noah A. Smith. 2011. Semi-supervised frame-semantic parsing for unknown predicates. In *Proceedings of the ACL: Human Language Technologies*.

Andrew B. Goldberg and Xiaojin Zhu. 2006. Seeing stars when there aren't many stars: graph-based semi-supervised learning for sentiment categorization. In *Proceedings of the Workshop on Graph Based Methods for NLP*.

Amarnag Subramanya and Jeff Bilmes. 2008. Soft-supervised text classification. In *EMNLP*.

Amarnag Subramanya, Slav Petrov, and Fernando Pereira. 2010. Graph-based semi-supervised learning of structured tagging models. In *EMNLP*.

Partha Pratim Talukdar, Joseph Reisinger, Marius Pasca, Deepak Ravichandran, Rahul Bhagat, and Fernando Pereira. 2008. Weakly supervised acquisition of labeled class instances using graph random walks. In *EMNLP*.

Tutorial Abstracts of ACL 2012, page 6,

Author Index